HEAVEN
FACT OR FICTION?

THEODORE C. DANSON SMITH

ISBN 0 7132 0039 1

B. McCall BARBOUR
28 George IV Bridge, Edinburgh, EH1 1ES, Scotland

HEAVEN
FACT OR FICTION?

By
THEODORE C. DANSON SMITH,
Th.D., Litt.D., F.M.E.

Author of Signs of the Saviour's Return,
From the Rainbow to the Rapture,
Basic Fundamentals of the Faith,
and Terrors to Come

B. McCall BARBOUR
Edinburgh, Scotland

DEDICATION

I dedicate this little book to my sister
GRACE
who has been my colleague and co-worker in the literature ministry since our teenage days.

© First published May 2000

CONTENTS

Introduction		Page 6
Chapter 1	**THE REVEALED PLACE**	Page 8
Chapter 2	**THE RANSOMED PEOPLE**	Page 16
Chapter 3	**THE ROYAL PERSON**	Page 24
Chapter 4	**THE RAREST PROSPECT**	Page 34
Chapter 5	**THE RECOGNITION PROMISED**	Page 41
Chapter 6	**THE RULING POSITION**	Page 49
Chapter 7	**THE REQUIRED PROPENSITY**	Page 57
Chapter 8	**THE REMORSELESS PUNISHMENT**	Page 67
Epilogue		Page 75

INTRODUCTION

In days of uncertainty, confusion and much false teaching, it is important to find out FACTS. This little book sets out to present some FACTS concerning HEAVEN. In no way does the author intend to speculate, but finds all his facts in the written and infallible Word of God - the Bible. Much more could be written on this subject, but some basic facts are here presented to comfort the true Christian, and to help show the Way to heaven to those who are not yet saved.

Every living person will at some time or other leave this scene of time. They need to know about their future and make the necessary preparations now. No one dies like a beast, for born within us all is the awareness of eternity, and the fact that this earthly life is but a short preparation for a greater and much longer one to follow. The great question is "WHERE WILL YOU SPEND ETERNITY?"

In days of science fiction we have to denounce all who say that heaven is fiction. The Creator of our universe is the One Who said "I go to <u>prepare</u> a place for you." Heaven - plenty of facts, but no fiction!

Chapter 1

THE REVEALED PLACE

Heaven! What a thought! Where is it? Is it a real place? Such are the questions that some may be asking. It is so easy to think that one, when they die, automatically goes to the place which people refer to as HEAVEN, but, can one be certain? Is it perhaps the figment of someone's imagination which inspires the belief in such a place? People know with assurance that there is something after this life, but the great question is "What?".

When we turn to the Bible - God's infallible Word - we find that Heaven is truly a real place. The Son of God - the Lord Jesus Christ - told His closest followers in John's Gospel chapter 14 verses 1 to 6 - "Let not your heart be troubled: ye believe in God, believe also in Me. In My Father's house are many mansions: if it were not so, I would have told you. I go to prepare a place for you. And if I go and prepare a place for you, I will come again, and receive you unto Myself; that where I am, there ye may be also. And whither I go ye know, and the way ye know. Thomas saith unto Him, Lord, we know not whither Thou goest: and how can we know the way? Jesus saith unto him, I AM THE WAY, THE TRUTH AND THE LIFE: no man cometh unto the Father, but by Me". There is but one way.

Those followers of the Lord Jesus Christ were aware that before very long He would be leaving them. Here, in no uncertain terms, the Saviour spelt out the way to Heaven. HE is the only way to Heaven. That wonderful place most certainly is real!

In our present society many people think that it is charitable to permit the belief that there are many ways to Heaven, but there is definitely only one way and that way is through faith in the Lord Jesus Christ Who came to this world and lived and gave His life that men and women, boys and girls would be able to enter Heaven. All other roads lead to hell and a lost eternity.

What do we know about Heaven? Well, it is a <u>revealed place</u>. The Lord Jesus Christ revealed some details to us. He is at present finishing His preparations. It is the Father's House. It is not somewhere on earth where the spirits of the Christian dead are contained. No, it is an actual place - both literal and physical, and for centuries the Saviour has been preparing this wonderful Home for all who are saved and trusting in Him.

Perhaps some reader is asking where this <u>revealed place</u> is. God's Word has the answer. Several heavens are mentioned in the Bible. Firstly, we have the heavens where the birds fly. Then, we have the heavens where the stars are situated, and, finally, we have the third heaven to which the apostle Paul refers in Second Corinthians 12 verses 2 to 4. Here Paul tells his readers that he was caught up there, and he heard words which he could not repeat. It was evidently such a fabulous experience that it affected his whole life. So, the first heaven is the atmospheric heaven. The second heaven is the planetary heaven, and the third heaven is the home of the redeemed.

The Revealed Place

Scripture tells us more about the <u>revealed</u> <u>place</u>. It is in the North. Someone may be asking - how do we know this? The Bible gives various indications about this. Heaven is located in a fixed position - "In the sides of the North". It is beyond the highest star. In the book of Isaiah chapter 14 verses 12 to 17 we find the record of the rebellion of Lucifer (Satan), and how the Lord put him down. In verse 15 we read - "Thou hast said in thine heart, I will ascend into heaven. I will exalt my throne above the stars of God: I will sit also upon the mount of the congregation, in the sides of the North". Satan intended placing himself above the Lord God, but he was immediately deposed and promised an eternity in hell.

Another interesting portion of the Bible is found in Psalm 75. In verse 6 of this Psalm we learn that "promotion cometh neither from the east, nor from the west, nor from the south". It goes on to state in the following verse that the Lord is the judge Who promotes or judges people. Neither the East, nor the West, nor the South is His place. His home is in heaven - in the North! Surely, that may account for people talking about going UP to heaven! The North is up, is it not?

Where is Heaven? It appears that the <u>revealed</u> <u>place</u> is in the North. We know it as the Gloryland where the Lord Jesus Christ lived and was worshipped by the holy angels before He left there to come to this earth of ours to make full atonement for man's sin. It must have been "empty" when His matchless presence was absent for thirty three years. Yet, He was the only One Who could pay the price for us. His precious, sinless blood - literal blood - was shed at Calvary that we might have life - eternal life and a guaranteed home in Heaven. The Lord Jesus said emphatically - "I go to prepare a place".

There is a fine old hymn which asks a rather pertinent question -

"Will you meet me at the fountain
When I reach the gloryland?
Will you meet me at the fountain?
Shall I clasp your friendly hand?

The Revealed Place

Other friends will bid me welcome,
Other loving voices cheer:
There'll be music at the fountain -
Will you, will you meet me there?"

The <u>Revealed</u> <u>Place</u> has many beautiful dwellings in it. Paul says in 1 Corinthians 2.9 - "Eye hath not seen, nor ear heard, neither have entered into the heart of man, the things which God hath prepared for them that love Him". The Lord Jesus Christ told His friends in John 14.2 - "In My Father's house are many mansions: if it were not so, I would have told you. I go to prepare a place for you." What a wonderful promise this is to the child of God! Heaven is the "Father's house". Dr. John R. Rice has written - "Doubtless the Saviour, facing the torments of Gethsemane, His betrayal, His desertion by the disciples, His trial before the Sanhedrin and Pilate, and the agonies of the cross, was Himself sweetly comforted by remembering the happy place to which He was going and where He would prepare many mansions for His Own redeemed. Certain it is that countless millions have learned not to let their hearts be troubled as the sweet realisation of

Heaven as an actual place has come home to their hearts."

In Heaven, pain will be gone for ever. There will be no sickness, no sadness, no sorrow and no death. There will be no blindness, no deafness and no other physical limitations or handicaps. All the inhabitants will have perfect health.

Dr. R.A. Torrey, the great evangelist, said about Heaven - "It is a place of incomparable external, as well as internal, beauty. This appears from such descriptions as we have in the 21st and 22nd chapters of the last book in the Bible. The God of the Bible is a God of beauty. There will be in Heaven the perfection of beauty; perfection of form, colour, sound and odour. The beauty that is to be is necessarily indescribable!"

In 1st Timothy 3.16 we read - "God was manifest in the flesh, justified in the Spirit, seen of angels, preached unto the Gentiles, believed on in the world, received up into glory". Here, we find the <u>revealed</u>

place is called "glory". Heaven will not only reveal the glory of God; it will also be the Glory Land - a place of unending joy and gladness. The Christian can truthfully sing the words of the beautiful hymn -

"When all my labours and trials are o'er,
And I am safe on that beautiful shore,
Just to be near the dear Lord I adore,
Will through the ages be glory for me.

When by the gift of His infinite grace
I am accorded in heaven a place,
Just to be there, and to look on His face,
Will through the ages be glory for me.

Friends will be there I have loved long ago;
Joy like a river around me will flow;
Yet, just a smile from my Saviour, I know
Will through the ages be glory for me.

Oh, that will be glory for me,
Glory for me, glory for me,
When by His grace, I shall look on His face,
That will be glory, be glory for me."

Chapter Two

THE RANSOMED PEOPLE

The people who will dwell in heaven with the Lord and His angels are all those who have put their trust in the Lord Jesus Christ and His finished work at Calvary. When He yielded up His life on the Cross, we are told He shouted the words "It is finished". People standing by thought that He was finished, but the wonderful fact is that there at Calvary He completed the work for which He had come to earth. He had finished the work of atonement for sin. He had accomplished the work of redemption. The Bible says in Hebrews 9 verse 22 "Without shedding of blood is no remission". Precious, sinless blood had to be shed to make atonement for our sin, and the Lord Jesus Christ, the only begotten Son of God, did just that. In the words of Charles Wesley's great hymn -

The Ransomed People

"He breaks the power of cancelled sin,
He sets the prisoner free;
His blood can make the foulest clean;
His blood avails for me."

All who have been washed in that precious blood will have a home in heaven. All who have been ransomed by the Lord will be there.

It will be a place of great fellowship, for all will be believers. No unsaved ones will ridicule the gospel. No lost souls will be there to disturb the peace and tranquillity. The <u>ransomed</u> <u>people</u> consists of all blood-washed sinners. Many good-living people will not be there. Others who are religious will be missing. Many ministers and so-called Christian leaders will not be there, for only those who have been redeemed by the blood of Christ will be allowed into heaven. Revelation chapter 19 verses 1 to 6 describes a little of what will happen in Heaven. Verse 6 says "I heard as it were the voice of a great multitude, and as it were the voice of many waters, and as the voice of mighty thunderings, saying, Alleluia: for the Lord God omnipotent reigneth". There will be a vast multitude there – all of them <u>ransomed people</u>. Furthermore, in Revelation chapter 7 verse 9 the Bible says "Lo, a great multitude, which no man could number, of all nations, and kindreds, and people, and tongues, stood before the throne, and before the Lamb, clothed with white robes, and palms in their hands." People from every tribe and nation, people from all the ages - in fact every soul who has put their trust in the Saviour will be in heaven. This is <u>home</u> for God's people! Are you one of His?

There are people today who believe wrongly that there are many roads to heaven, but there is only one way - the Lord Jesus Christ. He emphatically made it clear in these words - "No man cometh unto the Father, but by Me". Revelation 21 verse 27 says - "There shall in no wise enter into it (heaven) any thing that defileth, neither whatsoever worketh abomination, or maketh a lie: but they which are written in the Lamb's book of life". Every human being is a sinner, for we are born with sinful natures. The Bible says in Romans 3 verse 23 - "All have sinned, and come short of the glory of God". Also, in Romans 6.23 we read - "The wages of

The Ransomed People 19

sin is death; but the gift of God is eternal life through Jesus Christ our Lord". The apostle Peter addressed the religious leaders of his day - the Jewish Sanhedrin, and his words in Acts 4.12 state very clearly the only way to heaven - "Neither is there salvation in any other: for there is none other name under heaven given among men, whereby we must be saved". Salvation is in and through Christ alone! Isaiah 53 verse 6 says "The Lord hath laid on Him (the Lord Jesus Christ) the iniquity of us all". Peter, in his First Epistle chapter 2 verse 24 states that the Lord Jesus "His Own self bare our sins in His Own body on the tree".

Heaven will have room for the <u>ransomed</u> <u>people</u> only. All others will be lost for ever and ever. The true child of God has so much to anticipate. Heaven is known as "the Father's house". All of His own blood-bought children will be there. None will be absent or missing. Even those who may have wandered or strayed will be present, for salvation is entirely of grace and not of works.

John Jasper, former slave and one of America's greatest preachers of the nineteenth century was speaking to his congregation one day on Heaven and the joys which will await on the other side. He tried to describe its beauties with his vivid imagination, but he suddenly became overcome. He could say no more and waved his people to go home, but they sat on and waited. They were enthralled. G.B. Vick records what happened as eventually he managed to find these words. "Brothers and sisters, when I think of the glory which shall be revealed in us, I can visualise that day when old John Jasper's last battle has been fought and the last burden borne. I can visualise that day when this tired servant of God shall lay down his burdens and walk up to the battlements of the City of God. Then, as I stand outside the beautiful gate, I can almost hear the Mighty Angel say - 'John Jasper, you want your shoes?' I'm gonna say, 'Course I want my shoes, my golden slippers, to walk the gold-paved street of the city of God, but not now'. Then, I can hear him say, 'John Jasper, don't you want your robe?' And, I'm gonna say, 'Course I want my robe, that robe of fine linen, clean and white, which is the righteousness of the saints, but not now.' Then, the Mighty Angel will say, 'John Jasper, you want your crown?' I shall say, 'Course I want my crown - all the reward that's coming to me, this poor black servant of the Lamb, but not now'. Then, the Angel will say - 'John Jasper, wouldn't you like to see Elijah, the great prophet, who called down fire from Heaven? Wouldn't you like to shake hands with John, the beloved disciple, who leaned on the Master's breast at the Last Supper? Wouldn't you like to shake hands with Paul, the great apostle to the Gentiles, the greatest church establisher and soul winner of all time?' I'll say, 'Course, Mighty Angel, I want to know and shake hands and commune with those saints of God who have won the incorruptible crown. Yes, I have some loved ones over here too that I want to see, but not now. First, I want to see Master Jesus. I want to see Him first of all'!"

As ransomed people, every born-again Christian should keep that ambition before him.

Heaven will also have many angel inhabitants. In Matthew chapter 18 verse 10 the Lord Jesus Christ told His hearers not to despise little children, and He stated warningly that "in heaven their angels do always behold the face of My Father Which is in heaven". In the words of D.L.Moody - "Those who have never known what it is to transgress, those who have never known what it is to be disobedient, and those who have obeyed Him from the very morning of creation will be there". They will join the <u>ransomed</u> <u>people</u> in worship and adoration of the Saviour.

Our lips today may sing the words which then will be reality:

"Praise, my soul, the King of heaven;
To His feet thy tribute bring;
Ransomed, healed, restored, forgiven,
Who like thee His praise shall sing?
Praise Him! Praise Him!
Praise the everlasting King."

For the <u>ransomed</u> <u>people</u> Heaven is their ultimate and permanent Home. As Dr. John R. Rice says - "This world is only an anteroom of the next. This short life is incidental compared with eternity. This world is not home to the Christian. Here we are only sojourners, temporary dwellers in a foreign land. Our citizenship is in Heaven. Our thoughts should dwell lovingly and longingly on that sweet home of the departed saints, and of our Saviour,

The Ransomed People

and of our Heavenly Father". For the born-again believer the words of my father, J. Danson Smith, in his little poem entitled "We're Going Home" are most appropriate:

"We're going Home! We're going Home!
No more o'er barren wastes to roam;
And if the way seem long we've trod,
We're going Home to Heaven and God.

What if the way be oft-times rough -
We're going Home - that is enough!
How sweet the welcome that awaits
Our entry at Heaven's pearly gates!

What hallowed bliss within its walls!
What peaceful rest within its halls!
No sense of sin, no sound of strife -
Just radiant, joyful, endless life.

What fellowship we then shall share!
How wonderful the frames we'll wear
In that dear realm - Heaven's Homing-place!
And all through Christ's redeeming grace."

Chapter 3

THE ROYAL PERSON

Revelation chapters 4 and 5 give us a peep into Heaven, and here we find the <u>Royal</u> <u>Person</u> - the King of kings - the Lord Jesus Christ!   Chapter 4 verses 2 to 4 states "And immediately I was in the spirit: and, behold, a throne was set in heaven, and One sat on the throne. And He that sat was to look upon like a jasper and a sardine stone: and there was a rainbow round about the throne, in sight like unto an emerald. And round about the throne were four and twenty seats: and upon the seats I saw four and twenty elders sitting, clothed in white raiment; and they had on their heads crowns of gold." The remainder of this chapter describes the worship of the King, and it concludes in verse 11 - "Thou art worthy, O Lord, to receive glory and honour and power: for Thou hast created all things, and for Thy pleasure they are and were created".

The Royal Person

In chapter 5 again there is a scene of worship and adoration. The Lamb slain is here described as "the Lion or the tribe of Juda", and He is all-powerful. John the Baptist introduced the Lord Jesus Christ by saying in John 1.29 - "Behold the Lamb of God, Which taketh away the sin of the world". The Lord Jesus Christ came in order to pay the price for sinners. He went to the Cross of Calvary not as a martyr, but as a willing substitute for you and for me. His head was crowned with thorns. His side was pierced. His precious blood was shed that poor lost sinners might be saved and cleansed from all sin. Three days later He rose from the grave in victory! Is it any wonder that in Revelation chapter 5 verses 12 and 13 millions cry out "Worthy is the Lamb that was slain to receive power, and riches, and wisdom, and strength, and honour, and glory, and blessing. And every creature which is in heaven, and on the earth, and under the earth, and such as are in the sea, and all that are in them, heard I saying, Blessing, and honour, and glory, and power, be unto Him that sitteth upon the throne, and unto the Lamb for ever and ever". The <u>Royal</u> <u>Person</u> - the Lord Jesus Christ - the only Saviour - will be worshipped and adored by millions for all eternity.

In Isaiah chapter 33 verse 17 we read - "Thine eyes shall see the King in His beauty". This will be a staggering experience - perhaps too much for ordinary mortal eyes to behold. However, the child of God by then will have "put on immortality" as the apostle Paul says in 1 Corinthians 15.53. The apostle John tells us in Revelation chapter 4 verse 3 that there is "a rainbow round about the throne, in sight like unto an emerald". Ezekiel in chapter 1 verse 28 also speaks of this rainbow. He was given a glimpse of it, for he says - "As the appearance of the bow that is in the cloud in the day of rain, so was the appearance of the brightness round about. This was the appearance of the likeness of the glory of the Lord". It will be dazzling, and a most thrilling experience for the Christian to see their Saviour for the first time.

The well-known writer, George Goodman, said of the <u>Royal</u> Person - "We are come to the city of the Living God, the Heavenly Jerusalem, that is the metropolis that will be the centre of His rule.... We see Him now crowned with glory and honour but He waits at present till 'His enemies be made His footstool' (Hebrews

10.13). Then, He shall reign". And, as the Bible tells us, He will reign on earth for a thousand years. As the great old hymn says -

"Jesus shall reign where'er the sun
Doth his successive journeys run;
His kingdom stretch from shore to shore,
Till moons shall wax and wane no more."

In Acts chapter 7 we read about Stephen, the first martyr. After he was arrested and taken before the High Priest and council, he made a tremendous speech, and as it drew to a close we read in verses 55 and 56 that he "being full of the Holy Ghost, looked up steadfastly into heaven, and saw the glory of God, and Jesus standing on the right hand of God. And said, Behold, I see the heavens opened, and the Son of man standing on the right hand of God". He saw the <u>Royal Person</u>, and as he was cast out of the city and was stoned to death, he went instantly to be with his Saviour. What a welcome awaited him!

D.L. Moody, the great evangelist, said - "we will be

able to see Christ in His glory then. Though the moon be confounded and the sun ashamed, yet will we see Him as He is (Isaiah 24.23). This is what will make heaven so happy." Then, in the Glory, we shall see the Word of God in Philippians 2 verses 9 to 11 fulfilled - "Wherefore God also hath highly exalted Him, and given Him a name which is above every name; That at the name of Jesus every knee should bow, of things in heaven, and things in earth, and things under the earth; and that every tongue should confess that Jesus Christ is Lord, to the glory of God the Father".

The <u>Royal</u> <u>Person</u> - the Lord Jesus Christ - left all His glory behind for thirty three years in order to rescue and redeem poor lost human beings. He left His home. He left the Father's side. He left the worship and adoration of millions of angels that we might have life-eternal life! The apostle John wrote in 1st John 5 verses 11 and 12 - "This is the record, that God hath given to us eternal life, and this life is in His Son. He that hath the Son hath life: and he that hath not the Son of God hath not life". That life - eternal life - and a perfect salvation is available today to all who will

The Royal Person

repent of their sin and ask the Saviour into their hearts. The hymnwriter penned these lovely lines -

"Redemption! Oh, wonderful story -
Glad message for you and for me:
That Jesus has purchased our pardon
And paid all the debt on the tree.

From death unto life He hath brought us,
And made us by grace sons of God;
A fountain is opened for sinners;
Oh, wash and be cleansed in the blood!

Accept now God's offer of mercy;
To Jesus, oh hasten today;
For He will receive him that cometh,
And never will turn him away.

Believe it, O sinner, believe it;
Receive the glad message - 'tis true;
Trust now in the crucified Saviour:
Salvation He offers to you."

May it be that many people reading this message will turn in repentance and seek the Saviour. His wonderful promise in John 6.37 states - "Him that cometh to Me I will in no wise cast out".

As our minds travel to Heaven we cannot but think of the <u>Royal</u> <u>Person</u> Who will be there. Every child of God who dies goes instantly to Heaven. This is certain, for the apostle Paul stated in Philippians chapter 1 that he had a problem. In verse 23 he said - "For I am in a strait betwixt two, having a desire to depart, and to be with Christ; which is far better". However, the Lord needed him still on earth to work and witness for Him.

When one goes on a journey by car, train or coach we usually anticipate meeting someone at the other end. As Christians, saved by God's grace and washed in the precious blood, we should look joyfully to that moment when we shall see our Saviour. Sadly, many fail in this aspect, and live for self only.

The <u>Royal</u> <u>Person</u> is not only resident in Heaven. He is

The Royal Person

coming some day soon to collect His bride. That body is the true Church - all who are redeemed. Many church members, elders, ministers and leaders will be left behind as they are only religious. RELIGION saves no one. We need a RELATIONSHIP - a personal relationship with the Lord Jesus Christ. The Bible says in 1st Thessalonians chapter 4 verses 16 and 17 - "The Lord Himself shall descend from heaven with a shout, with the voice of the archangel, and with the trump of God: and the dead in Christ shall rise first: Then we which are alive and remain shall be caught up together with them in the clouds, to meet the Lord in the air: and so shall we ever be with the Lord". The picture is clear. The Lord Jesus Christ will come to the air, and from all over the world the living believers will be caught up to meet their King. At the same moment, every Christian who has died will be raised from the dead and given a new body, and they also will meet the Saviour. What a glorious moment that will be, when from every tribe and nation, and from every century since Calvary, people of all ages will meet the <u>Royal Person</u>! To quote the words of a well-known hymn - "What a gathering of the ransomed that will be"!

Seven years after that, the <u>Royal</u> Person will return to the earth to conquer and reign. The world's armies at that moment will be in Israel fighting the world's last battle - Armageddon. The heavens will open, and suddenly the whole world will see the King coming! Revelation chapter 19 verses 11 to 16 describes the scene - "And I saw heaven opened, and behold a white horse; and He that sat upon him was called Faithful and True, and in righteousness He doth judge and make war. His eyes were as a flame of fire, and on His head were many crowns; and He had a name written, that no man knew, but He Himself. And He was clothed with a vesture dipped in blood: and His name is called The Word of God. And the armies which were in heaven followed Him upon white horses, clothed in fine linen, white and clean. And out of His mouth goeth a sharp sword, that with it He should smite the nations: and He shall rule them with a rod of iron: and He treadeth the winepress of the fierceness and wrath of Almighty God. And He hath on His vesture and on His thigh a name written, KING OF KINGS, AND LORD OF LORDS". As the enemies of the Lord are destroyed and vast numbers of soldiers are killed, the

The Royal Person

Antichrist, who is the soon-coming world ruler, and his associate, the False Prophet, will be "cast alive into a lake of fire burning with brimstone" (verse 20). Revelation chapter 20 verse 15 reminds us that all who are not saved will also experience the same destination.

Keith L. Brooks indicates that Israel then will have found her King. No unbelieving Israeli will ever see Heaven, but when the <u>Royal</u> <u>Person</u> comes to the earth to conquer and reign for a thousand years Israel will receive the One Whom they rejected. He says - "Looking upon Him, they will discover that their Deliverer is none other than the One pierced so long ago at Calvary. Their city of Zion (Jerusalem) shall be recognised as the capital of all the earth".

"Lo He comes with clouds descending,
Once the Lamb for sinners slain;
Thousand thousand saints attending
Swell the triumph of His train.
Hallelujah! Hallelujah!
Jesus comes, and comes to reign!"

CHAPTER 4

THE RAREST PROSPECT

When one has travelled this scene of time with all its problems, difficulties, upheavals, joys and sorrows, pains and partings, there is a day coming which will be the <u>Rarest</u> <u>Prospect</u>. John, in his first Epistle chapter 3 verse 2 says - "Beloved, now are we the sons of God, and it doth not yet appear what we shall be: but we know that, when He shall appear, we shall be like Him; for we shall see Him as He is". "Like Him" are two most inspiring words! One day soon the Christian will be like the Lord Jesus Christ!

D. L. Moody said - "Just to see Him will be more than sufficient for all the sacrifices we can possibly make for Him. But, even more, we will become like Him when we see Him. In heaven, Jesus, the Saviour of the world, will be there and we will see Him face to face. It won't be the pearly gates, it won't be the jasper walls

The Rarest Prospect

and the streets paved with transparent gold that will make it Heaven for us. It is being with God. We will be in the presence of the Redeemer. We will be for ever with the Lord".

Through reading the Bible the Christian is instructed how to live. Yet, so many fail, and others falter, and some fall. The apostle John says to the children of the Father - "Beloved, now are we the sons of God.... and when He shall appear, we shall be LIKE HIM! All our imperfections, faults and failures will vanish. All physical disabilities and bodily illnesses will be gone for ever, for we shall be "like Him", and He is perfect! In the first place, He created the world, and it was a beautiful place. John chapter I verse 3 says - "All things were made by Him; and without Him was not anything made that was made". Nothing evolved, for the Lord Jesus Christ, the only-begotten Son of God, created this world of ours. Sadly, sin spoiled it. But, when we reach the Glory Land we shall be perfect! My good friend, John W. Peterson, wrote these lovely lines:

"Like Him some day we'll surely be!
Like Him when His dear face I'll see!
Like Him for all eternity!
Some day we'll surely be like Jesus.

No more pain or earthly sickness,
Twisted limbs will be restored;
No more growing old or dying,
We'll have bodies like the Lord!"

We are reminded of a passage in 2nd Thessalonians chapter 1 verses 7 to 12. This was written to comfort people who were being persecuted. Verse 10 says - "He shall come to be glorified in His saints, and to be admired in all them that believe". Keith L. Brooks says of this verse - "He is not simply to be glorified BY His saints, but IN His saints. All the universe will then see Him in His people and every eye shall see Him (Revelation 1.7). We shall be like Him. This is the highest glory of Jesus. It is not the Shekinah cloud, the dazzling throne, or the angelic hosts. It is those whom He has made to share in His nature and who shall reign with Him in glory".

The Rarest Prospect

George Goodman, who taught the Word many years ago, spoke of the change we shall undergo in order to be "like Him". He said - "What intellectual enlargement awaits the saints in the land where we shall know even as we have been known! But, better than all increase of knowledge, dearer than advance of capacity, more precious than all perfection.... will be this simple, satisfying, longed-for consummation - 'they shall see His face' (Revelation 22.4)".

The <u>Rarest</u> <u>Prospect</u> is that one day soon the believer will be "like Him". In Philippians chapter 2 verse 7 we are reminded that the Lord Jesus Christ was "made in the likeness of men" in order to accomplish our redemption, but the day will soon be here when every true child of God will be "like Him". How wonderful! Heaven is the dwelling place of God, and of every soul that has been saved by God's grace and born again of God's Holy Spirit. That is guaranteed! Dear reader, is that your prospect? If not, you can repent of your sin now and accept the Lord Jesus Christ as your personal Saviour. Otherwise, you are as Ephesians chapter 2 verse 12 tells us - without Christ, without God and with no hope.

Dr. W. Graham Scroggie reminds the true child of God that the Lord Jesus Christ wanted His followers to see His glory and partake of it. He directs us to John chapter 17 verse 24 - "Father, I will that they also, whom thou hast given Me, be with Me where I am; that they may behold My glory". He then goes on to say - "God's glory, that is, all that God is, is in Christ, and the prayer that we may eternally behold it will be answered. In Heaven rapturous adoration will never cease. 'They have no rest day and night, saying, Holy, Holy, Holy, is the Lord God Almighty, Who was, and is, and is to come' (Revelation 4.8). God infinite and absolute is made real to us in Christ; His ineffable transcendence is embodied in the Glorified Man, and our worship of Him will be our worship of God. This Beatific Vision will make us what we then shall be". "Like Him!" The <u>Rarest</u> <u>Prospect!</u>

In this life the Christian may endeavour to "be like Jesus" as the old chorus goes, but when we reach Heaven there is no question but we shall be "like

The Rarest Prospect

Him". What a privilege! What an honour! What a rare prospect! Meantime, all who are saved must wait, watch and work. My father penned another lovely poem as follows:

THAT COMING MORNING

"We wait that Morning - morning of surprises -
When we with eyes immortal shall behold
The wondrous home which He is now preparing,
Of which so little meanwhile hath been told.

'Twill far surpass all human comprehension;
Sublimest dreams - to paint it - ever fail;
And human minds - most brilliant and most daring -
Find words - to tell of heaven - of no avail.

We there shall see the Saviour Who hath loved us
And washed us from our sins in His Own blood;
The mystery and the marvel of His passion
Will then, at last, be fully understood.

And loved ones will be at that holy "rapture",
Whom we have sadly lost, and cherished long;
And saints, who great became, and who have blest us,
Will be 'mongst those we'll see in that great throng.

Oh, wondrous morning, when the Heavenly Bridegroom
Will come and take His purchased Bride away!
Oh, wondrous bliss - unsullied and unending -
Heaven's peerless home, and life's Eternal Day!"

J. Danson Smith

Chapter 5

THE RECOGNITION PROMISED

The question is often asked - "Shall we know one another in Heaven?" When we turn to Scripture we find the answer is "Yes"! 1st Corinthians chapter 13 verse 12 states - "Now we see through a glass, darkly; but then face to face: now I know in part; but then shall I know even as also I am known". The apostle Paul makes it very clear that we ourselves shall be known, and, if so, we shall recognise and know others. In Mark chapter 9 we read about the Transfiguration of the Lord Jesus Christ. He was visited on the mountain top by Moses and Elijah and they talked together. Peter, James and John were present, and it is obvious from the Word of God that they knew and recognised Moses and Elijah without being told who they were. In Matthew chapter 22 verse 32 the Saviour answered a question from the Saducees by saying, "I am the God of Abraham, and the God of Isaac, and the God of Jacob.

God is not the God of the dead, but of the living".

W. E. Vine reminds us that there is recognition now of the departed. He says - "Recounting the experience of the rich man and Lazarus, the Lord makes clear the matter of recognition in the intermediate state. Lazarus was in the place which the Lord figuratively calls 'Abraham's Bosom'. It was a place of bliss, separated by an impassable gulf from that region of Hades to which the rich man had gone. His recognition of Abraham continued".

Today we can envisage the scene that awaits the Christian. Heaven with its millions of inhabitants will be a wonderful reality. In that marvellous place we shall see and recognise in the vast throng the saints of all ages. Rahab - the once loose-living woman - will be there because of her faith. Enoch, who was taken Home without dying, will be seen. Noah, who faithfully preached and warned multitudes for 120 years, will be present. Paul and John and the other great apostles will be recognised. Martin Luther, John Knox and other great Reformers will be seen and

The Recognition Promised

admired. Bishops Latimer and Ridley, who perished for their faith, and every born-again person will be in that happy home. So, <u>recognition</u> is <u>promised</u>!

As Hebrews chapter 11 verse 13 says of the departed believers - "These all died in faith." That word "faith" reminds us of the tremendous need to have true faith in the finished work of Christ. He died in OUR place. He paid the price of OUR sin. Is He today OUR Saviour? That is the vital matter! Each person needs salvation or they will never be in Heaven.

Fanny Crosby, whom the Lord inspired to write so many wonderful hymns speaks the truth in these wonderful lines:

"Redeemed, how I love to proclaim it,
Redeemed by the blood of the Lamb;
Redeemed through His infinite mercy,
His child and for ever I am.

Redeemed and so happy in Jesus,
No language my rapture can tell;
I know that the light of His presence
With me doth continually dwell.

I think of my blessed Redeemer,
I think of Him all the day long;
I sing, for I cannot be silent,
His love is the theme of my song.

I know I shall see in His beauty
The King in Whose law I delight;
Who lovingly guardeth my footsteps
And giveth me songs in the night.

I know there's a crown that is waiting
In yonder bright mansion for me;
And soon, with the spirits made perfect,
At home with the Lord I shall be."

Robert Lee tells the story of a Christian lady who asked her learned husband if we would know one another in Heaven. His answer was plain and to the point. "Why, of course we shall! We know one another here, and surely you do not imagine that we shall be bigger fools up there than we are here". Robert Lee went on to comment - "Certainly it would not be Heaven - that truly human and blessed abode of which Christ is the centre - if our individual personalities were annihilated, and we were unable to recognise one another....Heaven will be a life of unbroken love. Reunion rests upon the permanence of personality. Personality is an eternal possession"!

Bishop J.C. Ryle confirms this by stating - "Saints in heaven shall know one another. They shall have the same body and the same character that they had on earth - a body perfected and transformed like Christ's in His transfiguration, but still the same body; a character perfected and purified from all sin, but still the same character. In the moment that we who are saved shall meet our friends in heaven, we shall at once know them, and they will at once know us".

The great apostle Paul wrote in his first letter these encouraging words to the young church in

Thessalonica - "What is our hope, or joy, or crown of rejoicing? Are not even ye in the presence of our Lord Jesus Christ at His coming?" (1st Thessalonians 2.19). Paul expected to see and recognise these converts when the Lord Jesus comes again.

We can say with certainty that the born-again Christian will definitely know and recognise their friends in the Glory Land. <u>Recognition</u> is <u>promised</u>!

Edwin R. Miles many years ago penned the words of a poem entitled "Our Friends in Heaven" and it goes as follows:

"Sometimes we wonder what our friends are doing
Within the precincts of the home above;
One thing is certain; they are now enjoying
The fullness of the heavenly Father's love.

They're now with Christ - their best Friend and Companion-
At home at last with Him; no longer here;
At rest from all life's cares and tribulations,
They now enjoy a far more glorious sphere.

The Recognition Promised

Set free from all the frailties of the body,
In spirit now they worship and adore
The ONE Who loved and gave Himself to save them,
More freely and more fully than before.

Inside the pearly gates they now are living,
Within the Four Square City bright and fair;
The wondrous street of gold they now are treading,
And drinking of the river flowing there.

Amid the glories our beloved are sharing,
The best is surely that they see His face,
They are in His blest presence, all adoring -
They are at rest, secure in His embrace.

Until we meet our loved ones, now in Heaven,
We'll seek to tread the path they long had trod;
Assured our Saviour will be ever with us,
'Till we ourselves arrive at home with God.

"He faileth not" must be our constant watchword,
He knows, and loves, and cares, our strength and stay;
He goes before us, guiding and protecting,
He careth for us each succeeding day.

So let us onward go along life's journey,
Strong in the grace of Christ, our Saviour dear;
Returning thanks for all His many mercies,
And daily watching for Him to appear."

Chapter 6

THE RULING POSITION

The Bible clearly indicates the establishment in space- somewhere above the earth - of a tremendous city - the New Jerusalem. The Apostle John tells us in Revelation chapter 21 verse 2 - "I John saw the holy city, new Jerusalem, coming down from God out of heaven, prepared as a bride adorned for her husband". Again, in verse 10 of the same chapter, he states - "And he carried me away in the Spirit to a great and high mountain, and showed me that great city, the holy Jerusalem, descending out of heaven from God". In all the verses that follow he describes this great city. It is apparently cube shaped, for in verse 16 we learn that the length, breadth and height are each fifteen hundred miles. Our finite minds may find this rather difficult to comprehend, but with the Lord as Designer He will be doing a new thing! The Bible says in Matthew chapter 19 verse 26 - "With God all things are possible".

It will be a place of unutterable magnificence. Revelation chapters 21 and 22 in part give one some idea of its beauty. In the new Jerusalem there will be no need for the sun nor any artificial light, for chapter 21 verse 23 tells us - "The city had no need of the sun, neither of the moon, to shine in it: for the glory of God did lighten it, and the Lamb is the light thereof". Verse 3 of the following chapter informs us that "there shall be no more curse". This confirms what the prophet Isaiah wrote in chapters 35 and 60. Then, Revelation chapter 21 verse 25 states that "there shall be no night there". This reminds us of the tragedies of darkness - sin, drunkenness, violence and many other evils. Darkness can cause depression, but the Psalmist reminds us in Psalm 27 verse 1 that "The Lord is my light and my salvation; whom shall I fear?" Darkness can also speak of death and bereavement. Revelation chapter 21 verse 4 tells us - "God shall wipe away all tears from their eyes; and there shall be no more death, neither sorrow, nor crying, neither shall there be any more pain: for the former things are passed away". So, the Lord's dear people can anticipate joy and happiness as well as health and strength! Isaiah chapter 25 verse 8 says - "He will swallow up death in victory;

and the Lord God will wipe away tears from off all faces". What a wondrous time it will be when the Lord Jesus Christ is ruling over all the earth!

This great City - the New Jerusalem - is the <u>Ruling Position</u> of the future for planet earth. It will be from this city that the Lord Jesus Christ alone with His bride, the True Church, will rule. Matthew Chapter 19 verse 28 speaks of the Saviour sitting on "the throne of His glory" with saints of God associated with Him in government. Peter, in his Second Epistle chapter 3 verse 13 writes of "new heavens, and a new earth, wherein dwelleth righteousness". John reminds us in Revelation chapter 11 verse 15 that the day is coming when there will be a tremendous announcement - "The kingdoms of this world are become the kingdoms of our Lord, and of His Christ; and He shall reign for ever and ever". When the child of God reads this, he wants to cry out "Hallelujah"!

The prophet Zechariah in chapter 14 describes the return of the Lord Jesus Christ to this earth when He shall come in power and great glory. He will conquer the world's armies which will then be assembled in Israel, and He will establish His rule. Verse 16 states - "It shall come to pass, that every one that is left of all the nations which came against Jerusalem shall even go up from year to year to worship the King, the Lord of hosts, and to keep the feast of tabernacles". The Jewish nation and all the peoples of the earth will see their King, for verse 9 says - "The Lord shall be king over all the earth". His <u>Ruling</u> <u>Position</u> will be established. He will not persuade men, for His power will be such that no man or government will succeed in opposing Him. As Dr. C. I. Scofield remarks - "The moral characteristics of the kingdom are to be righteousness and peace. The meek, not the proud, will inherit the earth. Longevity will be greatly increased. The knowledge of the Lord will be universal; ferocity will be removed; absolute equity will be enforced; and outbreaking sin visited with instant judgment; while the enormous majority of earth's inhabitants will be saved".

The <u>Ruling</u> <u>Position</u> of the Saviour will guarantee Satan's permanent removal, for he will be chained in a bottomless pit for a thousand years as Revelation 20

The Ruling Position

verse 2 states. Later, he will be consigned for ever to the Lake of Fire.

The New Jerusalem is often referred to as "the Holy City", and this is correct, for it will be the ultimate goal of our Redeemer. As Paul says in Ephesians chapter 1 verse 4 the Lord's desire is that His people "should be holy and without blame before Him in love".

Andrew Borland, speaking of the Ruling Position, has said - "The throne of God and of the Lamb are there. In Revelation chapter 4 the vision is of the throne of God in all its unsullied governmental splendour, a splendour of holiness which repels everything that is not in the strictest harmony therewith. In chapter 5 the Lamb approaches that throne, associates Himself therewith, and now the ideas are combined, and within the Eternal City there is seen the 'throne of God and of the Lamb' - one throne, one centre of government with a dual character".

The Bible is full of references to the Throne, and Revelation itself has many verses dealing with the

Throne. It is obvious that the Throne is a position of rule, and therefore the King of all the earth will exercise His authority worldwide.

John Bloore helpfully describes the New Jerusalem in these words - "This is the city of my God....Jerusalem, the foundation of peace. Upon that foundation God builds that blessed and glorious system of things which will constitute our eternal sphere of habitation. It is peace made by the Blood of the Cross. On this basis reconciliation is effected in perfect agreement with the fullness of the Godhead. That foundation shall never be shaken, never moved, the peace of that city never broken, its order never disturbed; it abides for ever in its beauty, freshness, holiness, and glory - God's eternal tabernacle among men".

The prolific writer, Dr. Herbert Lockyer, gives a description of the New Jerusalem as follows: "The city John so fully describes is to be the eternal home of Christ and His Own, whose glorified bodies will correspond to Christ's...Others, of course, will also share His glory (Revelation chapter 21 verses 24 to 26), but the Church

The Ruling Position

will be as a wife at home. God's eternal home is to be in this capital city of the New Creation, more resplendent than any renowned capital in the world today. This is the centre of divine presence and government in the universe....The gates of the city will never be shut. Police will be unnecessary to guard the city dwellers since there will be no more thieves. Nations can come and go. All that accompanies sinful darkness disappears....Our eyes will behold the King in all His beauty".

The prophet Isaiah says in chapter 2 verse 4 - "He shall judge among the nations, and shall rebuke many people: and they shall beat their swords into plowshares, and their spears into pruninghooks: nation shall not lift up sword against nation, neither shall they learn war any more." The Bible also states in Micah chapter 4 verse 7 - "The Lord shall reign over them in Mount Zion from henceforth, even for ever".

God's law and His Word will be the basis for the <u>Ruling</u> <u>Position</u> worldwide. The prophet Isaiah foresaw all this when he wrote in chapter 9 verse 6 - "The government shall be upon His shoulder: and His name shall be called Wonderful, Counsellor, The mighty God, The everlasting Father, The Prince of Peace".

The King surely is coming, and the whole earth will benefit enormously from His rule. We can surely rejoice with the hymnwriter who penned these lovely lines -

"He is coming, our Lord and Master,
Our Redeemer and King;
We shall see Him in all His beauty,
And His praise we shall sing.

He shall gather His chosen people,
Who are called by His name;
And the ransomed of every nation
For His Own He shall claim.

Hallelujah! Hallelujah!
He is coming again;
And with joy we will gather round Him
At His coming to reign."

Chapter 7

THE REQUIRED PROPENSITY

In this chapter we shall look at the <u>Required Propensity</u> which would enable anyone to go to Heaven. Revelation chapter 21 verse 27 emphasises - "There shall in no wise enter into it anything that defileth, neither whatsoever worketh abomination, or maketh a lie: but they which are written in the Lamb's book of life". Here it is very clear that in order to enter Heaven one must be saved. "The Lamb" is the Lord Jesus Christ, and in His "book of life" are entered the names of every soul who has repented of their sin and put their trust in the precious, cleansing blood of the Lamb. John the Baptist, in John chapter 1 verse 29 , introduced the Lord Jesus Christ as "the Lamb of God, Which taketh away the sin of the world". He came into the world in order to pay the price of our sin. Every human being is born a sinner. Adam - the first man - was created by God, but, sadly he <u>chose</u> to sin, thus bringing condemnation on every human being. As Romans chapter 5 verse 12 says - "By one man sin entered into the world, and death by sin; and so death passed upon all men, for that all have sinned".

Writing also in the same chapter the apostle Paul proclaims this glorious message - "God commendeth His love toward us, in that, while we were yet sinners, Christ died for us". Do we know and understand the reality of this? Have we ourselves experienced the love of God and salvation through the Lord Jesus Christ? If not, we can repent now and accept God's Gift - the Lord Jesus Christ as our personal Saviour, and thus experience the cleansing power of His precious blood. Someone may ask why stress the blood of Christ, and the answer simply is found in Hebrews chapter 9 verse 22 where the writer says - "Without shedding of blood (there) is no remission" - no forgiveness! Christ's blood was shed in order that we might have life - eternal life. John chapter 3 verse 16 proclaims - "God so loved the world, that He gave His only begotten Son, that whosoever believeth in Him should not perish, but have everlasting life". God's love extends to

The Required Propensity

every human being, but not everyone wants that love.

The <u>Required</u> <u>Propensity</u> is salvation, and salvation is only available through the Saviour. Religion cannot save. Good works are useless. Living a perfect life is impossible. Only the Lord Jesus Christ can provide us with salvation. The Bible says in 1st Timothy chapter 1 verse 15 - "Christ Jesus came into the world to <u>save</u> sinners". Can we search our hearts and ask ourselves if we are saved? In 1st John chapter 5 verses 11 and 12 the Bible assures any doubters - "This is the record, that God hath given to us eternal life, and this life is in His Son. He that hath the Son hath life; and he that hath not the Son of God hath not life". Each one of us either has experienced the salvation of God, or is still a lost soul. The Word of God says in Romans chapter 6 verse 23 - "The wages of sin is death; but the gift of God is eternal life through Jesus Christ our Lord". We can receive God's wonderful Gift, the Lord Jesus Christ, now - if we wish!

This is the <u>Required</u> <u>Propensity</u> for entering Heaven.

The following lines should speak to every reader:

THE BOOK OF LIFE

"There's a book which God is keeping,
And within its pages fair
Many blood-washed names are entered;
Is thy name recorded there?

Pure and stainless are its pages,
Kept above with sacred care;
It shall stand through endless ages;
Is thy name recorded there?

Traced perhaps, in many albums,
Is the earthly name you bear;
But within 'Life's Book eternal',
Is thy name recorded there?

Earthly books and earthly writings
All alike decay shall share;
But, God's Book time cannot alter;
Is thy name recorded there?

The Required Propensity 61

Time is fleeting, swiftly fleeting,
So to trifle do not dare;
Seek to have thy sins forgiven,
And thy name recorded there.

Soon the judgment day is coming,
Then, delay not to prepare,
Lest thy name should be found wanting
'Mid the names engraven there."

Dr. John R. Rice wrote - "Jesus is the way to Heaven. He is not part of the way to Heaven; He is the whole way. He is not one of the ways; He is the only way. The dear Lord Jesus is the one, sweet, simple way to Heaven. I am so glad it is Jesus and not someone whom I couldn't trust to let me in. But, Jesus, He loves me and died for me. I know I can trust Him. Jesus is the Way to Heaven!" He goes on to add - "Christ has prepared a home for you in Heaven. He wants you there. I believe you want to go there. Then put your trust in Jesus Christ just now, and have it settled for ever! You can then expect Him to take you home to the mansions He has prepared for those who trust Him.

Reader, why don't you just now shut the door and get down on your knees and tell Jesus Christ that you will trust Him now to be your Saviour, trust Him to forgive all your sins, trust Him to change your heart, and rely on Him to take you to heaven? Or, sitting in that chair, or lying in that bed, where you are, right now, trust Him with all your heart. The moment you wholly trust Him you will have eternal life".

When we trust the Saviour our names are instantly entered in His book of life. We can be sure that once there we become His for ever. His death at Calvary made full atonement for us. My father, J. Danson Smith, penned these lovely lines:

"Written in heaven! Oh, wonderful story -
Written in heaven - my name is now there!
What shall it mean when, in wonderful glory,
I shall behold it in letters so fair.

Written in heaven, but not through my merit;
I could not scribe it - no title had I;
Only through Christ - through His death I inherit
Place in the record unfading on high.

Written in heaven, through wondrous redemption;
Thus my rejoicing - small wonder indeed;
Free from the law - and from death, blest exemption -
Knowing my name there my Saviour doth read.

Written in heaven! Christ died to redeem us;
Only through Him are our names written there.
God did so love us, and fondly esteem us,
He bore our guilt that we might His bliss share".

The Word of God states clearly in Romans chapter 10 verse 13 -"Whosoever shall call upon the name of the Lord shall be saved". We need to note that word "whosoever", for that means just what it says! Every soul who truly and sincerely repents and asks the Lord to save them will be saved, and thus made ready for Heaven. Not only did the Saviour die for our sins, He also rose for our justification, proving that God the Father, as well as justice, was satisfied. As the great old hymn puts it -

"Full atonement! Can it be?
Hallelujah! What a Saviour."

The <u>Required</u> <u>Propensity</u> clearly is <u>salvation!</u> The great and godly first Bishop of Liverpool - Dr. J. C. Ryle - said - "Heaven itself would be no heaven if all sorts of characters got there. There could be no order and no happiness in such a heaven.... Ask yourself whether you shall be found among the many who shall 'sit down in the kingdom of heaven'. The question demands an answer. I charge you to give your soul no rest until you can answer it in a satisfactory way. Time is passing quickly away, and the world is growing old. The signs of the times ought to set us all thinking. The 'distress of nations' seems to increase every year. The wisdom of statesmen seems utterly unable to prevent wars and confusion in every direction. The progress of art, and science and civilisation appear entirely powerless to prevent the existence of enormous moral evils. Nothing will ever cure the diseases of human nature but the return of the Great Physician, the Prince of Peace, the second coming of the Lord Jesus Christ Himself".

In closing this chapter I quote again a poem of my father - J. Danson Smith. It asks a powerful question -

IS YOUR NAME WRITTEN THERE?

"Is your name written there
In the Lamb's Book of Life?
When you leave this old world
With its sin and its strife?
Will they find your name there -
'Mongst the ransomed of God -
In the Lamb's Book of Life,
Through the Lamb's precious blood?

When life here is finished
To some realm we must go -
To the mansions of bliss
Or the dungeons below;
For the soul never dies -
It for ever must last,
When life, as we know it,
For ever has passed.

Let me ask once again -
Is your name written there?
Will you be in Heaven's bliss
Or in endless despair?
You have nothing to do
But the Saviour accept,
But woe unto you
If His name you reject."

Chapter 8

THE REMORSELESS PUNISHMENT

The title of this chapter may sound terrible, but it expresses the sobering fact that <u>all</u> who reject the Lord Jesus Christ as Saviour or are simply quite indifferent will never see Heaven or dwell in that wonderful place. In Ephesians chapter 2 verse 12 God's Word states that such people are "without Christ....having no hope, and without God". What a situation!

The truth is, as John chapter 3 verse 17 says - "God sent not His Son into the world to condemn the world, but that the world through Him might be saved". God's desire is our personal salvation, but His gift of salvation He will not force upon us. That gift is there to be accepted or rejected. John chapter 3 verse 36 tells us - "He that believeth on the Son hath everlasting life: and he that believeth not the Son shall not see life; but the wrath of God abideth on him". Notice the last phrase of that verse - "the wrath of God abideth on him". Yes, we have a choice as individuals! We either accept God's remedy or experience His wrath. Psalm 9 verse 17 proclaims - "the wicked shall be turned into hell". In Matthew chapter 23 verse 33 the Lord Jesus Christ said to the religious leaders of His day - "Ye serpents, ye generation of vipers, how can ye escape the damnation of hell?" Religion can never save. Only the Lord Jesus Christ can, and sadly in our generation most religious leaders fail to preach the way of salvation. As a result, multitudes are going to hell for ever and ever. In Luke chapter 16 the Saviour tells the story of two men - the rich man and Lazarus. The day came when the rich man passed away and his body was buried. Where was he? The Lord Jesus Christ said- "In hell he lift up his eyes, being in torments". He was in the place of the unsaved dead awaiting his final judgment at the Great White Throne where he will be sentenced to spend all the ages to come in hell - the lake of fire - the place of never-ending torment. In Revelation chapter 20 verses 12 to 15 we have the picture of what is ahead for every unsaved person - "I saw the dead, small and great, stand before God; and

The Remorseless Punishment

the books were opened: and another book was opened, which is the book of life; and the dead were judged out of those things which were written in the books, according to their works. And the sea gave up the dead which were in it; and death and hell (hades) delivered up the dead which were in them: and they were judged every man according to their works. And death and hell (hades) were cast into the lake of fire. This is the second death. And whosoever was not found written in the book of life was cast into the lake of fire". Fact or fiction? Heaven and hell are both very real!

The <u>Remorseless</u> <u>Punishment</u> will be carried out for one reason -rejecting God's way of salvation. Do you, dear reader, wish to experience the wrath of a holy God? If not, I urge you to repent <u>now</u> and accept the Lord Jesus Christ as your personal Saviour. He left His glory in Heaven and came to this earth that we might have life.

Heaven is a real place, and so is hell! Revelation chapter 21 verse 27 gives this solemn warning - "There shall in no wise enter into it (Heaven) any thing that defileth, neither whatsoever worketh abomination, or maketh a lie: but they which are written in the Lamb's book of life". In the same chapter, verse 8 tells us - "The fearful, and unbelieving, and the abominable, and murderers, and whoremongers, and sorcerers, and idolaters, and all liars, shall have their part in the lake which burneth with fire and brimstone: which is the second death". "The second death" - eternity in hell is the alternative to the second birth. The Lord Jesus Christ told the most religious man of His day - "Ye must be born again". We are "born again" only when we repent of our sin and ask the Saviour in. When He saves us, His precious blood, shed at Calvary, is that which cleanses us. First John chapter 1 verse 7 tells us- "The blood of Jesus Christ His Son cleanseth us from all sin". There is no sin too great that cannot be covered by this promise except that of rejecting the Lord Jesus Christ as one's Saviour.

The <u>Remorseless</u> <u>Punishment</u> of the lost will go on for ever. The Bible makes this so clear. Some hope that hell will only be temporary, but the Word of God uses the phrase "tormented day and night for ever and

The Remorseless Punishment

ever". Is that your prospect? Paul wrote about the lost ones in Second Thessalonians chapter 1 verses 8 and 9 - "in flaming fire taking vengeance on them that know not God, and that obey not the gospel of our Lord Jesus Christ: Who shall be punished with everlasting destruction from the presence of our Lord, and from the glory of His power".

Hell was prepared for Satan and the angels who rebelled against the Lord, and God does not wish human beings to go there. The Bible says in Second Peter chapter 3 verse 9 - God is "not willing that any should perish, but that all should come to repentance". If we offered someone a very special gift and they refused to accept it, or were totally indifferent, how would we feel? God's great gift is a full and free salvation through His only-begotten Son, the Lord Jesus Christ. Yet, very few accept that wonderful gift!

Hell is a place of separation from God. It also separates the lost from the saved. In many families today there is only perhaps one Christian. All the rest will end in hell. In that place of <u>Remorseless</u>

Punishment there will be the vilest of company - sinners of all kinds who rejected the Saviour. Dr. Herschel Ford in a message on hell continued as follows: "Now let's go to heaven for a minute, seeking relief from the fumes of hell. We meet a former thief up there and he says 'I was on the way to hell. I could almost feel the flames. But as I hung on a cross, Jesus snatched me as a brand from the burning. I am here because I put my trust in Him'. Then, we meet Paul who says 'I was on the way to hell. I was putting Christians to death. But one day Jesus appeared to me on the Damascus Road and I gave myself to Him. I am here because I trusted Him'. Then, we meet the Philippian jailer, who says, 'I was on the way to hell, but one night I had two preachers in my jail. At midnight there was an earthquake and I thought my life was over. But, these preachers told me about Jesus. I put my faith in Him that wonderful night, and now I am here because I trusted Him'."

Dear reader, if you do not belong to the Lord, will you not repent now and ask the Lord into your heart and thus receive eternal life? In Ezekiel chapter 33 verse 11

The Remorseless Punishment

the Lord says - "I have no pleasure in the death of the wicked; but that the wicked turn from his way and live". God's earnest desire is our salvation, but He will not force that gift upon us. He says in His infallible Word in Second Corinthians chapter 6 verse 2 - "Now is the accepted time; behold, now is the day of salvation". The choice is yours. Turn or burn! Repent or perish! Heaven or hell!

The words of a great hymnwriter leave us with a great challenge:

"Time is swiftly gliding by,
Death and judgment draweth nigh,
To the arms of Jesus fly:
Be in time!
Oh, I pray you count the cost,
Ere the fatal line be crossed,
And your soul in hell be lost:
Be in time!

Sinner, heed the warning voice,
Make the Lord your final choice,
Then all heaven will rejoice:
Be in time!
Come from darkness into light;
Come, let Jesus make you right;
Come and start for heaven tonight:
Be in time!"

EPILOGUE

Heaven - Fact or Fiction? The suggestion of "fiction" is totally ridiculous. In these few pages we have mentioned a few of the glorious "facts". Heaven is a real place. Heaven is for real people - those who have been saved by God's grace. Heaven's preparations are almost complete. Any day now the Saviour will come and take His waiting people Home. There will be no more tears - just endless joy as we live with the Saviour for ever - the One Who loved us and gave Himself for us. Sadly, hundreds of millions alive today will never reach Heaven. The Lord Jesus Christ spoke of two roads - the narrow road of salvation, through faith in Christ, and the broad road leading to destruction. On which road are you?

Heaven will be fabulous - far more wonderful than any pen could write or tongue can tell. The Lord Jesus Christ Who created our world is now finishing His work on our eternal home. Dr. Curtis Hutson tells the story of a young boy who was out with his grandfather one dark night. "The sky was deep blue, and it seemed like a million stars were on parade. The little boy pulled at his grandfather's coat and said, 'Grandpa, Grandpa, if Heaven is so beautiful on the outside, what must the inside be like?'"

We conclude this simple message with the words of another lovely hymn, a verse of which we have quoted earlier:

"Will you meet me at the fountain?
For I'm sure that I shall know
Kindred souls and sweet communion,
More than I have known below;
And the chorus will be sweeter
When it bursts upon my ear,
And my heaven seem completer
If your happy voice I hear.

Epilogue

Will you meet me at the fountain?
I shall long to have you near
When I meet my loving Saviour,
When his welcome words I hear.
He will meet me at the fountain,
His embraces I shall share;
There'll be glory at the fountain -
Will you, will you meet me there?"

Unsaved friend, - "Believe on the Lord Jesus Christ, and thou shalt be saved" (Acts 16.31). TODAY is your opportunity, for one day soon there will not be one Christian left on earth. Then, it will be too late! "Seek ye the Lord while He may be found" (Isaiah 55.6).

BIBLIOGRAPHY

Brooks, Keith L., **Prophecies Of The Epistles**
Los Angeles,
American Prophetic League, 1942.

Hutson, Curtis, **Heaven,**
Murfreesboro, Sword Of The Lord
Publishers, 1981.

Moody, D. L., **Heaven – How To Get There,**
Chicago, Moody Press.

Pickering, Henry, **Heaven - The Home Of The Redeemed**
Glasgow, Pickering and Inglis

Rice, John R., **Bible Facts About Heaven,**
Murfreesboro, Sword Of The Lord
Publishers, 1940.

Ryle, J. C., **Shall We Know One Another In Heaven,**
Kilkeel, Mourne Missionary Trust.

Bibliography

Scofield, Dr. C. I., **The Scofield Reference Bible**
New York, Oxford University Press, 1917.

Scroggie, W. Graham, **What About Heaven,**
Glasgow, Pickering and Inglis, 1940.

Smith, J. Danson, **One Hundred Best Loved Poems**
Edinburgh, B. McCall Barbour, 1970.

Stanton, Don, **Where Will You Spend Eternity**
Roelands, Maranatha Revival Crusade, 1998

OTHER BOOKS BY THE SAME AUTHOR

SIGNS OF THE SAVIOUR'S RETURN

The world is inundated with problems, wars, famine, and many other ills. This book shows that the only answer to these problems, is the return of the Lord.

FROM THE RAINBOW TO THE RAPTURE

The whole topic from Genesis to Revelation is covered in this book. It shows how God has had a plan for man down through the ages. It will make you think.

BASIC FUNDAMENTALS OF THE FAITH

This covers a range of topics very important in these days of apostasy. It deals with the Blood, Blessed Hope, Separation etc.

TERRORS TO COME

This book is written in a challenging manner, and it has an abundance of appeals to the unsaved. A book about the last days. This book will change your viewpoint on the last days.